Outstanding Early Years Provision in practice

by Nicola Scade

Contents

Published by Practical Pre-School Books, A Division of MA Education Ltd, St Jude's Church, Dulwich Road, Herne Hill, London, SE24 0PB.

Tel: 020 7738 5454 www.practicalpreschoolbooks.com

© MA Education Ltd 2014

Design: Alison Cutler **fonthill**creative 01722 717043

Disclaimer: Practitioners should take the recommended health and safety precautions with equipment provided and check beforehand for any allergies to materials. It is the responsibility of the practitioners to ensure that the resources provided are suitable for all children in the setting and necessary risk assessments should be carried out where appropriate.

ISBN 978-1-909280-59-5

Introduction

Who this book is for

It is often a challenge to continue to come up with exciting and inspiring areas of provision week after week. The aim of this book is to support all early years practitioners in creating a stimulating and awe-inspiring environment, by using what is already available in the setting. Being resourceful and creative with what you have also means you don't need to spend a fortune to create an exciting learning environment.

Especially when time is so precious for practitioners, this book avoids heavy-text descriptions and aims to **show how** to create outstanding continuous provision rather than **tell you how**, using concise text with an emphasis on bright and detailed pictures to inspire you to transform your learning environment.

This book is most suitable for those working in settings with children aged 3-5. The book would also be an ideal resource for students taking their PGCE course or any early years childcare course and EYTS qualification.

How to use this book

Each chapter will focus on a specific **area of provision;** showing how achievable it is to take it to the next level (the 'wow' factor) by utilising everyday resources and getting inside the mind of a child! The detailed photographs and captions show fresh and easy-to-replicate ideas.

Alongside the photos will be a list of **resources** needed, a challenge section with ideas on how to extend the provision, **observations** of children and **links** to the current Early Years Framework. There will also be **key questions** for you to ask yourself about each area of provision, enabling you to reflect on the needs of the child across all **seven areas of learning** and in relation to the characteristics of effective learning.

The **areas of learning tables** at the back of the book can help you plan these effectively.

Remembering the following simple points as you use this book will help you develop and improve your provision!

- Utilise what you already have

- Use 'the real thing' wherever possible

- Involve the children

- Continually check and monitor the effectiveness of the provision

- Ensure there are opportunities for extension and challenge.

Continuous provision

The resources, activities and experiences that are constantly available in a setting, both inside and outside, can be thought of as continuous provision.

This provision should ensure coverage across the seven areas of the curriculum and should be planned for in response to the developmental needs and interests of the children and with careful consideration of the characteristics of effective learning. These are outlined in the 2012 EYFS Framework.

"In planning and guiding children's activities, practitioners must reflect on the different ways that children learn and reflect these in their practice. The three characteristics of effective teaching and learning are:

- **Playing and exploring** – children investigate and experience things, and 'have a go';

- **Active learning** – children concentrate and keep on trying if they encounter difficulties, and enjoy achievements; and

- **Creating and thinking critically** – children have and develop their own ideas, make links between ideas, and develop strategies for doing things."

Statutory Framework for The Early Years Foundation Stage 2012, Section 1.10, P6 and 7.

This book will give you practical ideas on how to enhance this basic provision, creating activities which engage, stimulate and challenge.

And finally... Think like a child and have fun with your creations!

Chapter One: Exploration and investigation

Key Areas of EYFS developed in this chapter:

- Understanding the World

- Communication and Language

- Mathematics

- Expressive Arts and Design.

Activities for this chapter are:

- Archaeological dig
- Abracadabra!
- Arctic freeze
- How does your garden grow?
- We're going on a bug hunt
- Potions lab
- Marvellous magnets.

Useful resources for activities in this chapter:

- Magnifying glasses
- Assorted size rocks and stones
- Assorted size logs
- Plants and leaves
- Clipboards and notebooks
- Information books
- Assorted size containers
- Pipettes and test tubes.

Further provision ideas for this area:

- Freezing and melting
- Nature hunts
- Experiments – How do different ingredients react with each other?
- Investigating speed with cars and different materials
- Gardening
- Role play – science lab, archaeologists, explorers.

You will find specific links and resources for each activity in this chapter.

The real-life quotes from children in this chapter (and throughout the book) give a real insight into how each activity can contribute to children's learning across the seven areas of learning.

Real examples of learning include:

"If I find 5 pieces of treasure I will be get on the Pirate ship and take it to the good Pirate."

"It's melting all over my hand and dripping. It's too icy and cold."

" This plant has lines all over the leaves and so many colours."

Trapped inside an iceberg! How could you rescue the explorer?

Digging in the sand can become an archaeological quest to find the hidden remains of an ancient city!

Archaeological dig

 "I don't know what this is but I think it's from something scary because it's got pointy bones."

Setting up the provision

Method

Bury objects under the sand, making sure that some are visible to allow children to become curious about the activity. Position investigation resources around the edge of the tray.

Resources

- Sand
- Paint brushes
- Spades
- Magnifying glasses
- Old camera
- Head lamps or torches
- Clipboards and pens
- Collection of interesting rocks, fossils, logs, shells etc.
- Broken crockery.

Handy hints

- The paint brushes provide an excellent tool to enable children to delicately brush off the sand and examine their intriguing artefact.

- Fill the sand tray with lots of sand and bury many of the objects far below so that children to get the chance to dig deep!

- Natural materials such as logs and stones don't cost a penny. Ask children to help you build up a collection. The more unusual the better.

How does the activity enable children to develop and demonstrate the characteristics of effective learning?

Characteristic of effective learning	The enabling environment: Archaeological dig
Playing and exploring – engagement ● Finding out and exploring. ● Playing with what they know. ● Being willing to 'have a go'.	The activity is open-ended and multi-sensory. Children represent experiences through imaginative play, getting in character as archaeologists! The resources are new and exciting, encouraging children to 'have a go'.
Active learning – motivation ● Being involved and concentrating. ● Keeping trying. ● Enjoying achieving what they set out to do.	The natural resources are unusual and intriguing, enabling children to show high levels of fascination and maintain sustained concentration as they explore. Children have the opportunity to problem solve by themselves or with others, trying to uncover what the objects are and where they have come from.
Creating and thinking critically – thinking ● Having their own ideas. ● Making links. ● Choosing ways to do things.	Children have the opportunity to talk about and explain their knowledge, reflecting on how it links to previous experiences.

Carefully dusting off the mysterious artefact. All in a day's work for this budding Archaeologist!

How the activity can support children's development across the 7 areas of learning

Areas of Learning: Communication and Language

Children have the opportunity to:

- Develop their vocabulary as they are introduced to unfamiliar objects.
- Describe what they find.
- Ask questions.
- Explain own knowledge.

Areas of Learning: Physical Development

Children have the opportunity to:

- Handle small tools such as paintbrushes to dust off the sand.
- Dig deep.

Areas of Learning: Personal, Social and Emotional Development

Children have the opportunity to:

- Develop an inquisitive mind.
- Take into consideration the ideas of others.
- Develop the confidence to try new activities.

Areas of Learning: Literacy

Children have the opportunity to:

- Record what they discover.
- Read non-fiction books.

Areas of Learning: Mathematics

Children have the opportunity to:

- Compare shape, size and weight.

Areas of Learning: Understanding the World

Children have the opportunity to:

- Use their senses to explore new materials.
- Discuss where in the world the artefacts may come from.

Areas of Learning: Expressive Arts and Design

Children have the opportunity to:

- Draw what they find.
- Engage in role play.

  "Shall we make an X and bury it back, then we can find it again."

  "I'm digging in South Africa."

- Clipboards attached to the handles of the sand tray with string means that there are always opportunities to write and draw.

- Why not provide children with a real camera to take photos of the artefacts they uncover? The photos will provide an excellent stimulus for questions and conversation. They could also form the basis of a fascinating display.

Questions to help you extend the activity and to ensure challenge

Questions for you:

- Are there any non-fiction books that could support children's learning?

- Do children have access to key vocabulary relating to the activity?

- Could you create a lab to examine children's findings more closely? (Opportunity for an ongoing project.)

Questions for the children:

- Can you draw and label the things that you find?

- Can you describe the objects you find to a friend?

- Where in the world do you think these objects come from? Why do you think that?

Silky drapes and torches turn a collection of minibeasts into an enchanting magical den

Abracadabra!

Targeted areas of learning:
Expressive Arts and Design and Maths

Setting up the provision

Method
Create a cosy den with dark and silky fabrics. Dress the tray with interesting, sparkly material then layout your chosen objects to form a spooky potions lab. Find your way inside and explore!

Resources
- Small containers
- Scoops and spoons
- Torches
- Dark, silky material
- Magnifying glasses
- Torches
- Plastic minibeasts
- Minibeast non-fiction books.

Handy hints
- Material draped around an activity is inviting and provides a secure place from which to explore.

- Pegging material to a washing line above or attaching it to a nearby wall creates a backdrop or den for any activity.

- Opportunities for children to explore the effects of light are important wherever you have created a dark space.

Questions to help you extend the activity and to ensure challenge

Questions for you:
- Are there materials for children to record their own bug recipes or spells?

- Could you include bug stew recipe cards for children to follow, developing their counting, number recognition and addition skills?

How the activity can support children's development across the 7 areas of learning

Areas of Learning: Communication and Language

Children have the opportunity to:

- Describe and name the minibeasts.
- Make up their own spells and recipes.
- Develop a narrative to go alongside their play.

Areas of Learning: Physical Development

Children have the opportunity to:

- Strengthen their fine motor skills using tweezers and scoops.

Areas of Learning: Personal, Social and Emotional Development

Children have the opportunity to:

- Try out new activities and use new resources.
- Share resources.
- Maintain focus for a sustained period of time.

Areas of Learning: Literacy

Children have the opportunity to:

- Read non-fiction books.
- Write their own recipes and spells.

Areas of Learning: Mathematics

Children have the opportunity to:

- Sort, count and add the minibeasts.

Areas of Learning: Understanding the World

Children have the opportunity to:

- Explore and discuss similarities and differences
- Make links with previous experiences.
- Describe the effects of the torch.

Areas of Learning: Expressive Arts and Design

Children have the opportunity to:

- Engage in role play.
- Draw what they find.

Carefully inspecting the patterns on the bugs to decide how to sort them

- What resources could children use to collect the minibeasts? For example: tweezers, scoops.

Questions for the children:

- How could you sort the minibeasts?

- Can you explain what happens when you shine the torch on the material from close up and then from far away?

- How many different types of minibeasts are there? (Opportunities for drawing, tally charts, recording numbers etc.)

 "I'm going to make a bug pancake to feed the wicked witch because she is not very nice to the Princess."

 "I have lots of frogs, there isn't many snakes."

How does the activity enable children to develop and demonstrate the characteristics of effective learning?

Characteristic of effective learning	The enabling environment: Abracadabra!
Playing and exploring – engagement ● Finding out and exploring. ● Playing with what they know. ● Being willing to 'have a go'.	The activity is open-ended. Children can engage in imaginative play and develop narratives. The resources are exciting, containing a balance of familiar and new experiences.
Active learning – motivation ● Being involved and concentrating. ● Keeping trying. ● Enjoying achieving what they set out to do.	The draped material creates an enchanting den, allowing children to absorb themselves in the activity for a sustained period of time. Children have the opportunity to persevere when using small tools to collect the minibeasts.
Creating and thinking critically – thinking ● Having their own ideas. ● Making links. ● Choosing ways to do things.	Children have the opportunity to explore the effects of the torch, trying out new ways of doing things and making connections between cause and effect.

A cosy place from which to play and explore

It only takes a trip to the freezer to reach a frozen planet

Arctic freeze

Targeted areas of learning:
Understanding the World and
Communication and Language

Setting up the provision

Method

Fill assorted sized containers with water and then place them in the freezer over night to create icebergs. Add pipe cleaners or plants to create frozen trees. Trap play people or animals inside the ice to enhance the adventure!

Resources

- Plastic cups
- Empty well paint pallet
- Pipe cleaners
- Small plastic arctic animals
- Cotton wool
- Water
- Freezer (where possible).

Handy hints

- Using empty well paint palettes creates individual icebergs where you can conceal animals or explorers. Place a small plastic animal or play person in one of the wells of the pallet and then fill with water. Repeat until you have filled the tray. Place in the freezer overnight.

- To make the ice trees fill a plastic cup with water and add some green and silver pipe cleaners, half submerged in the water. Place in the freezer overnight. Snip the top of the cup and then pull away to reveal the frozen tree.

- Jelly moulds or large bowls make a good base in which to create a whole frozen island or snow globe. Submerge plastic animals, people, small leaves, branches and glitter for a 'wow' factor!

 "It's melting all over my hand and dripping. It's too icy and cold."

How does the activity enable children to develop and demonstrate the characteristics of effective learning?

Characteristic of effective learning	The enabling environment: Arctic freeze
Playing and exploring – engagement ● Finding out and exploring. ● Playing with what they know. ● Being willing to 'have a go'.	The activity is open-ended and multi-sensory. Children represent experiences through imaginative play, getting in character as artic explorers! The resources are intriguing, encouraging children to 'have a go'.
Active learning – motivation ● Being involved and concentrating. ● Keeping trying. ● Enjoying achieving what they set out to do.	The activity arouses immediate curiosity – How did the animals become trapped? How can we free them? How quickly will the ice melt?
Creating and thinking critically – thinking ● Having their own ideas. ● Making links. ● Choosing ways to do things.	Children can make decisions about the best way to achieve an end goal. Children can make and test their own predictions.

Investigate how long it takes for the ice to drip when it is warmed up in your hands

How the activity can support children's development across the 7 areas of learning

Areas of Learning: Communication and Language

Children have the opportunity to:
- Explain and discuss their ideas with others.
- Develop a narrative.
- Ask questions.
- Describe what they can see and feel.
- Develop new vocabulary.

Areas of Learning: Physical Development

Children have the opportunity to:
- Develop control over the handling of small resources.

Areas of Learning: Personal, Social and Emotional Development

Children have the opportunity to:
- Share resources.
- Ask for help when needed.

Areas of Learning: Literacy

Children have the opportunity to:
- Read and write adventure stories.

Areas of Learning: Mathematics

Children have the opportunity to:
- Problem solve.

Areas of Learning: Understanding the World

Children have the opportunity to:
- Comment on changes of state.
- Make and test predictions.

Areas of Learning: Expressive Arts and Design

Children have the opportunity to:
- Engage in role play.
- Create their own arctic scenes.

Questions to help you extend the activity and to ensure challenge

Questions for you:
- Are there investigation materials at hand for children to help excavate the frozen animals?

- Do children have access to key vocabulary relating to the activity?

- Are there relevant story books to hand that could support children develop a narrative to go alongside their exploration?

Questions for the children:
- How can we rescue the penguin from the ice?

- How can we speed up the melting process?

- Can you write a story about the arctic animals and how they got trapped in the ice?

How long will it take for the ice to melt and the animals to escape?

Add some investigation tools and your average garden becomes a mysterious and fascinating new land

How does your garden grow?

Setting up the provision

Method
Place investigation tools near to the plants outside, encouraging children to examine their environment.

Resources
- A variety of interesting plants to appeal to children's sense of sight, touch and smell
- Magnifying glasses
- Assorted size shells
- Clipboards and pens
- Plant identification books
- Senses flash cards
- Spades
- Watering cans
- Sketch books
- Scissors and magnifying pots for plant clippings.

Handy hints
- Supporting children to cut samples of different plants allows children to then closely inspect what they have found, perhaps in a microscope or by dissecting them.

 "This plant looks like it is from a Dinosaur land. I think they would have eaten it."

How the activity can support children's development across the 7 areas of learning

Areas of Learning: Communication and Language

Children have the opportunity to:

- Develop their vocabulary, learning the names of new plants.
- Ask questions.
- Describe what they observe.

Areas of Learning: Physical Development

Children have the opportunity to:

- Consider how plants and food can contribute to the growth and health of animals and humans.

Areas of Learning: Personal, Social and Emotional Development

Children have the opportunity to:

- Show care and concern for the world around them.

Areas of Learning: Literacy

Children have the opportunity to:

- Use reference books to check and develop their own knowledge.

Areas of Learning: Mathematics

Children have the opportunity to:

- Compare the size, shape and colour of plants and other objects.

Areas of Learning: Understanding the World

Children have the opportunity to:

- Show an interest in the world around them.
- Develop an understanding of growth, decay and changes over time.

Areas of Learning: Expressive Arts and Design

Children have the opportunity to:

- Make observational drawings and paintings.
- Use natural resources to make collages, perfumes, potions etc.

  "I love that smell of the lavender, can we cut some for the classroom?"

  "This plant has lines all over the leaves and so many colours."

- Planting as many herbs and scented plants as you can and allowing children to take cutting of these means that you have a ready-made perfume lab!

- Leaving other natural materials such as shells and fossils amongst the plants on a daily basis means that children can discover new things and build up their knowledge each day.

Questions to help you extend the activity and to ensure challenge

Questions for you:

- Are there opportunities to record what has been found, perhaps pictorially or in a chart?

- Do children have the opportunity to plant and nurture the garden themselves?

- Can children refer to non-fiction books as they explore?

Questions for the children:

- What kinds of animals would live here and why?

- Can you describe how a magnifying glass works?

- What could we do to find out more about these plants?

How does the activity enable children to develop and demonstrate the characteristics of effective learning?

Characteristic of effective learning	The enabling environment: How does your garden grow?
Playing and exploring – engagement ● Finding out and exploring. ● Playing with what they know. ● Being willing to 'have a go'.	The activity is open-ended and multi-sensory. Children are provided with tools to encourage and extend their exploration.
Active learning – motivation ● Being involved and concentrating. ● Keeping trying. ● Enjoying achieving what they set out to do.	The natural resources are intriguing, enabling children to show high levels of fascination and maintain sustained concentration as they explore. Children have the opportunity to find out more about the garden by using their senses, asking questions, using information books and talking with each other.
Creating and thinking critically – thinking ● Having their own ideas. ● Making links. ● Choosing ways to do things.	Children have the opportunity to talk about and explain their knowledge, making links between cause and effect and coming up with their own ideas. Leaving the investigation tools out on a daily basis allows children build on their knowledge week by week.

Listening for the sea and pretending that the 'magic shells' will take them there

A drop of rain transforms an ordinary bug hunt into an epic adventure

We're going on a bug hunt

Setting up the provision

Method

Bury plastic minibeasts amongst the real wildlife outside. Add some 'larger than life' creatures to build excitement.

Resources

- Outside area – soil, grass, plants, logs, stones
- Magnifying glasses and old cameras for play.
- Clipboards and pens
- Minibeast non-fiction and identification books
- Spades
- Old paint brushes for dusting the soil off logs and stones.

Handy hints

- The large plastic minibeasts help to add a sense of drama but there is nothing better than uncovering the real thing

- Dig deep, roll over logs and stones and see what can be found

- Wellies and umbrellas make a bug hunt all the more appealing!

- Get dirty!

 **"Let's do an insect register to see if they are all here."**

How does the activity enable children to develop and demonstrate the characteristics of effective learning?

Characteristic of effective learning	The enabling environment: We're going on a bug hunt
Playing and exploring – engagement ● Finding out and exploring. ● Playing with what they know. ● Being willing to 'have a go'.	The activity is open-ended and multi-sensory. Children represent experiences through imaginative play, getting in character as explorers! Different weather is utilised to enhance children's learning.
Active learning – motivation ● Being involved and concentrating. ● Keeping trying. ● Enjoying achieving what they set out to do.	The natural resources are unusual and intriguing, enabling children to show high levels of fascination and maintain sustained concentration as they explore. Children have a goal in mind.
Creating and thinking critically – thinking ● Having their own ideas. ● Making links. ● Choosing ways to do things.	Children can plan how to carry out their search. They can predict what they might find and use the tools and equipment in ways that they think are best suited to the task.

Working as a team to find as many different bugs as they can

How the activity can support children's development across the 7 areas of learning

Areas of Learning: Communication and Language

Children have the opportunity to:
- Describe, predict and plan.
- Listen and follow instructions.

Areas of Learning: Physical Development

Children have the opportunity to:
- Develop control handling new tools and equipment.
- Dig deep.
- Move heavy rocks and logs.

Areas of Learning: Personal, Social and Emotional Development

Children have the opportunity to:
- Show care and concern for the environment.

Areas of Learning: Literacy

Children have the opportunity to:
- Use reference books to check and develop their own knowledge.
- Draw and label the insects they find.

Areas of Learning: Mathematics

Children have the opportunity to:
- Record what they find in various ways, e.g. tally charts.

Areas of Learning: Understanding the World

Children have the opportunity to:
- Show interest in the local environment.
- Describe the effects of the weather.

Areas of Learning: Expressive Arts and Design

Children have the opportunity to:
- Make up songs and rhymes as they hunt.

Questions to help you extend the activity and to ensure challenge

Questions for you:
- Are there opportunities to record what has been found, perhaps pictorially or in a chart?

- Do children have the opportunity to plant and nurture the garden themselves?

- Are there opportunities to use cameras or film to record the adventure? Watching this back would provide an excellent stimulus for storytelling.

Questions for the children:
- What insects do you think we will find and where?

- Can you write some instructions for how to go on a bug hunt?

- How could we record what we find on our bug hunt?

Closely examining how the rain has affected a large spider's web

Filling and emptying or a colour explosion in the lab?!

Potions lab

Targeted areas of learning:
Expressive Arts and Design and Maths

 "When I pour from up high it's like a fountain."

Setting up the provision

Method

Add coloured paints to the water tray and fill assorted sized containers to different levels. Place a plank of wood across the water tray to create a level surface for the containers. Have a selection of other resources nearby for children to self select. For example: pipettes, sieves and funnels.

Resources
- Colored paints
- Assorted sized containers
- Funnels
- Scientist lab goggles
- Glitter
- Mixing utensils
- Pipettes and syringes (always without needles).

Handy hints
- Colored paint can transform an activity. From a crystal blue ocean to a green murky swap.

- Old white shirts make excellent lab coats.

- Sticking yellow and black hazard tape around the tray has a dramatic effect.

- Adding extracts of vanilla or peppermint for example to create fragrant water adds another dimension.

- Laminated A3 paper stuck on a wall nearby makes a splash proof resource for children to jot down any ideas as they are working. For example: ingredient lists, spells or words to describe their potions.

How the activity can support children's development across the 7 areas of learning

Areas of Learning: Communication and Language
Children have the opportunity to:
- Describe what happens when the colours mix.
- Talk through what they are doing.

Areas of Learning: Physical Development
Children have the opportunity to:
- Handle objects with control and safety.

Areas of Learning: Personal, Social and Emotional Development
Children have the opportunity to:
- Work collaboratively.

Areas of Learning: Literacy
Children have the opportunity to:
- Write ingredients lists.
- Draw and label the effects of their potion.

Areas of Learning: Mathematics
Children have the opportunity to:
- Explore capacity, weight and size.
- Recognise numbers.

Areas of Learning: Understanding the World
Children have the opportunity to:
- Comment on cause and effect.
- Describe patterns and change.

Areas of Learning: Expressive Arts and Design
Children have the opportunity to:
- Colour mix.
- Engage in role play.

"The colours are mixing to make a flying potion."

"It's so hard to fill this big tube, it's too heavy."

Questions to help you extend the activity and to ensure challenge

Questions for you:
- Is there key vocabulary hanging around the water tray?
- Could you use material to create an inviting backdrop behind the water tray?
- What else could you provide in the potions lab to develop children's fine motor skills?

Questions for the children:
- How many small beakers does it take to fill the large beaker?
- Can you read the numbers along the side of the jug? What are these numbers for?
- What will happen if we mix the red liquid and the yellow liquid together?

How does the activity enable children to develop and demonstrate the characteristics of effective learning?

Characteristic of effective learning	The enabling environment: Potions lab
Playing and exploring – engagement ● Finding out and exploring. ● Playing with what they know. ● Being willing to 'have a go'.	The activity is open-ended and multi-sensory. Children represent experiences through imaginative play, getting in character as scientists! The vibrant colours invite children to investigate.
Active learning – motivation ● Being involved and concentrating. ● Keeping trying. ● Enjoying achieving what they set out to do.	The variety of containers means that there are many different ways of doing things and many different outcomes. Children will have to use trial and error to manoeuvre the larger, heaver containers.
Creating and thinking critically – thinking ● Having their own ideas. ● Making links. ● Choosing ways to do things.	Children can set their own goals and adapt what they are doing accordingly. They can make and test predictions.

Exploring how the colours mix together and how to manoeuvre some of the heavier containers

Investigations are always more exciting when buried treasure is involved!

Marvellous magnetics

Targeted areas of learning:
Understanding the World and
Communication and Language

Setting up the provision

Method

Bury objects in the sand, placing assorted size magnets at the top ready for use. Position a treasure chest underneath or to the side of the sand tray.

Resources

- A collection of different types of magnets
- A collection of magnetic non-magnetic objects
- Clipboards and pens
- A treasure chest
- Sand.

Handy hints

- Designing a game where children can move a magnetic object through a piece of card can be achieved with a simply drawn maze, a pipe cleaner, a piece of card and a magnet. Watch children's faces as they realise they can move the pipe cleaner without touching it!

- Attaching magnets to the ends of small wooden poles and attaching paper clips to cardboard fish creates the opportunity to go fishing! Don't forget to add numbers, letters or words, for example, onto the fish.

- Your very own metal detector can be achieved by assembling junk modelling resources and attaching a strong magnet underneath. Take your new devices outside to discover new materials. Are they magnetic or not? Can the children explain why?

 **"If it isn't a magnet, it just doesn't stick on."**

How does the activity enable children to develop and demonstrate the characteristics of effective learning?

Characteristic of effective learning	The enabling environment: Marvellous magnetics
Playing and exploring – engagement ● Finding out and exploring. ● Playing with what they know. ● Being willing to 'have a go'.	The resources are new and exciting, encouraging children to 'have a go'. Using a balance of familiar and unfamiliar objects, children can play and explore, developing an understanding of new concepts.
Active learning – motivation ● Being involved and concentrating. ● Keeping trying. ● Enjoying achieving what they set out to do.	The resources are stimulating, enabling children to show high levels of fascination and maintain sustained concentration. Children have the opportunity to problem solve by themselves or with others, trying to uncover which objects are magnetic/non magnetic and how different materials compare.
Creating and thinking critically – thinking ● Having their own ideas. ● Making links. ● Choosing ways to do things.	Children have the opportunity to talk about and explain their own knowledge. They can start to investigate patterns.

Testing to see whether or not the object can go in the treasure chest

How the activity can support children's development across the 7 areas of learning

Areas of Learning: Communication and Language

Children have the opportunity to:

- Ask 'how' and 'why' questions.
- Use talk to connect ideas and explain own knowledge.

Areas of Learning: Physical Development

Children have the opportunity to:

- Demonstrate control over small equipment.
- Work safely with heavier objects.

Areas of Learning: Personal, Social and Emotional Development

Children have the opportunity to:

- Develop an inquisitive mind.
- Take into consideration other children's ideas.
- Develop the confidence to try new activities.

Areas of Learning: Literacy

Children have the opportunity to:

- Make treasure maps.

Areas of Learning: Mathematics

Children have the opportunity to:

- Problem solve.

Areas of Learning: Understanding the World

Children have the opportunity to:

- Investigate new materials and new concepts.
- Compare how materials are similar and different.

Areas of Learning: Expressive Arts and Design

Children have the opportunity to:

- Engage in role play.

"If I find 5 pieces of treasure I will be get on the Pirate ship and take it to the good Pirate."

"Can you help me use the big magnet outside?"

Questions to help you extend the activity and to ensure challenge

Questions for you:

- Can children extend their learning beyond the sand tray by using the magnets on objects around the room?

- Are there opportunities for children to record what they find out?

- Other than sand, what else could the objects be buried in?

Questions for the children:

- Can you fill the treasure chest with magnetic objects only?

- What else can you find in the room that is magnetic?

- Describe what happens when two magnetic objects are close together.

Jelly is everyone's favourite, so why not use it as a resource!

Chapter Two:
Fine motor skills and malleable materials

Activities for this chapter are:

- Precious gem search
- Snip, squash and squeeze
- Weaving
- Making perfume
- Shaving foam cakes
- Slime.

Useful resources for activities in this chapter:

- Tweezers and tongs
- Scissors and scoops
- Food colouring
- Glitter
- Assorted sized containers.

Key Areas of EYFS developed in this chapter:

- Physical Development

- Mathematics

- Expressive Arts and Design

- Communication and Language.

Further provision ideas for this area:

- Play dough
- Threading
- Porridge oats
- Small construction materials
- Workshop area
- Making sand paper letters and numbers.

You will find specific links and resources for each activity in this chapter.

Our independence and ability to access the world around us relies heavily on the development of our fine motor skills. The opportunities to strengthen these skills should be plentiful and fun.

Real examples of learning include:

"You have to squeeze it for the water to get in. You can make little drops with it."

"You have to move the letters carefully so they don't break up."

"I have decorated 3 cakes. I have given each one three cherries so it's fair."

Mix in your favourite colour to create the coloured slime of your choice!

Fine motor skills developed through a search for precious gems

Precious gem search

Targeted areas of learning:
Physical Development and Maths

Setting up the provision

Method
Spread a layer of sand onto a builder's tray and then decorate with coloured sand swirls, gems, open shells and tweezers.

Resources
- Shells that are open to create a dish
- Sand
- Glitter
- Plastic gem stones
- Tweezers and tongs.

Handy hints
- Adding a colour sticker to each shell means that children can collect and sort their gems.

 "If I slide it on a bit with my finger, then snap on to it with the tweezers then I can pick it up."

- Writing a number on each shell means that children can collect a given amount of gems for each shell, matching number to quantity.

- A dusting of coloured sand and shimmering glitter creates an activity that immediately invites you in.

- Once children are secure using tongs, see if they can master smaller tweezers.

Questions to help you extend the activity and to ensure challenge

Questions for you:
- Are there sand timers or stop watches for children to set their own timed challenges?

How the activity can support children's development across the 7 areas of learning

Areas of Learning: Communication and Language

Children have the opportunity to:
- Describe how the tools should be used.
- Negotiate how the activity should be carried out with others.

Areas of Learning: Physical Development

Children have the opportunity to:
- Develop their fine motor skills by handling. small gems and by using tongs and tweezers.

Areas of Learning: Personal, Social and Emotional Development

Children have the opportunity to:
- Work together to complete different challenges.

Areas of Learning: Literacy

Children have the opportunity to:
- Make treasure maps.

Areas of Learning: Mathematics

Children have the opportunity to:
- Sort by colour.
- Sort based on own criteria.
- Match number to quantity.
- Count.
- Create patterns.

Areas of Learning: Understanding the World

Children have the opportunity to:
- Discuss the different shells. Where are they from? What might have lived in them?
- Explore and explain the purpose of different tools.

Areas of Learning: Expressive Arts and Design

Children have the opportunity to:
- Create patterns.
- Engage in role play.

Getting to grips with tongs

- Are there numbers lines available to support children as they count?

Questions for the children:
- Can you collect the gems using just the tongs?

- How else could you sort the gems?

- How many gems can you collect in the large shell before the sand timer runs out?

 "We did team work to get all the gems in a pile in the middle."

"I have collected 5 square gems and 3 circle ones."

How does the activity enable children to develop and demonstrate the characteristics of effective learning?

Characteristic of effective learning	The enabling environment: Precious gem search
Playing and exploring – engagement ● Finding out and exploring. ● Playing with what they know. ● Being willing to 'have a go'.	Colourful and glistening resources will draw children to the activity.
Active learning – motivation ● Being involved and concentrating. ● Keeping trying. ● Enjoying achieving what they set out to do.	Children can persevere to use the tongs and tweezers successfully. Children can set their own challenges and try to improve on what they have achieved previously.
Creating and thinking critically – thinking ● Having their own ideas. ● Making links. ● Choosing ways to do things.	Children can use trial and error to work out and explain the best way of doing something.

Create a wow factor!

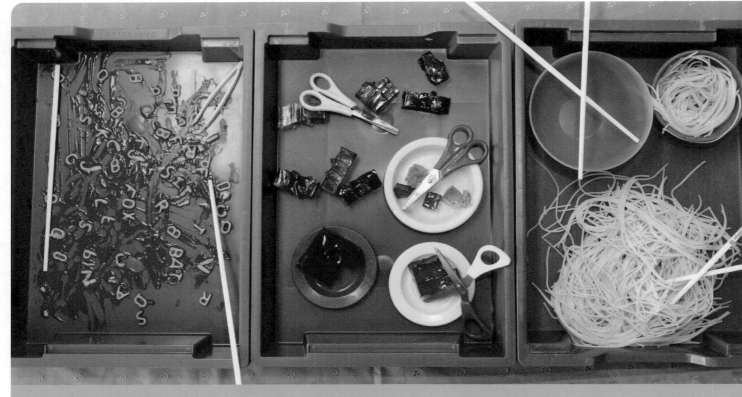

Raid the cupboards to see what awakens your senses!

Snip, squash and squeeze

Targeted areas of learning:
Physical Development
and Expressive Arts and Design

Setting up the provision

Method

Arrange malleable materials into three separate trays
with a variety of tools positioned ready to explore
each material. Jelly, spaghetti and pasta are particularly
useful resources to have to available.

Resources

- Alphabet and regular spaghetti
- Jelly
- Pasta
- Scissors
- Chop sticks
- Spoons and forks
- Plates and bowls.

Handy hints

- Adding washing up liquid to the food means that
  children will not be tempted to eat it!

- Access to both left handed and right handed scissors is
  crucial for all children to be able to access such activities.

- Cooked long spaghetti is an excellent resource for
  making shapes and pictures

- Adding food colouring to the spaghetti can make it
  even more appealing.

Questions to help you extend the activity and to ensure challenge

Questions for you:

- Are there both left-handed and right-handed
  scissors available?

- Are there opportunities for children to record how
  they have used their senses to explore the activity?

How does the activity enable children to develop and demonstrate the characteristics of effective learning?

Characteristic of effective learning	The enabling environment: Snip, squash and squeeze
Playing and exploring – engagement • Finding out and exploring. • Playing with what they know. • Being willing to 'have a go'.	The activity is multi-sensory. The opportunity to explore familiar foods in new ways is exciting and often amusing.
Active learning – motivation • Being involved and concentrating. • Keeping trying. • Enjoying achieving what they set out to do.	Children can persevere to use the scissors, chopsticks and other tools successfully.
Creating and thinking critically – thinking • Having their own ideas. • Making links. • Choosing ways to do things.	Children can use trial and error to work out and explain the best way of doing something. Children can express their own opinions. For example, on how something smells or feels.

Exploring and describing how the jelly feels and smells

How the activity can support children's development across the 7 areas of learning

Areas of Learning: Communication and Language

Children have the opportunity to:
- Describe the appearance, texture and smell of the resources.
- Explain and ask questions about the tools and how they should be used.

Areas of Learning: Physical Development

Children have the opportunity to:
- Develop control and skill using scissors and other one handed tools.
- Manipulate different materials to strengthen their fine motor skills.
- Show an awareness of how to use tools safely.

Areas of Learning: Personal, Social and Emotional Development

Children have the opportunity to:
- Share resources.
- Compare experiences with other children.
- Explain what they like and don't like and why.

Areas of Learning: Literacy

Children have the opportunity to:
- Recognise letters and sounds in the alphabet spaghetti.

Areas of Learning: Mathematics

Children have the opportunity to:
- Make patterns with the long spaghetti.
- Compare lengths of spaghetti.
- Compare the shape and size of the jelly pieces as they cut.

Areas of Learning: Understanding the World

Children have the opportunity to:
- Explore and explain the purpose of different tools.

Areas of Learning: Expressive Arts and Design

Children have the opportunity to:
- Use their senses to comment on appearance, texture and smell.

Questions for the children:
- Can you find the letters in your name?
- Can you find a long piece of spaghetti and a short piece?
- How could you describe the jelly?

 "You have to move the letters carefully so they don't break up."

"I found some letters in my name."

Identifying familiar letters and their corresponding sounds

A simple fence or a valuable resource?

Weaving

Targeted areas of learning:
Physical Development and Maths

Setting up the provision

Method
Have a basket of material cut into strips next to a fence.
Weave a couple of examples so that children can see the
end goal.

Resources
- Coloured fabric cut into long strips
- A fence.

Handy hints
- Leave examples of woven material on the fence so
  that children can see the end goal.

- Encourage children to work in partners to help secure
  the material as they are weaving.

 **"You need to push it
through and then get it
back out again."**

"It's easier when I use two hands."

Questions to help you extend the activity and to ensure challenge

Questions for you:
- Are there objects in the setting that could be used to
  show this weaving effect? For example, a wicker basket.

- Could you provide paper and colored pens for children
  to record the patterns they make with their weaving?

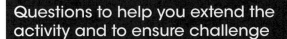

How the activity can support children's development across the 7 areas of learning

Areas of Learning: Communication and Language

Children have the opportunity to:

- Talk through what they are doing as they do it.
- Listen to and follow instructions.

Areas of Learning: Physical Development

Children have the opportunity to:

- Develop increasing skill and control over an object.

Areas of Learning: Personal, Social and Emotional Development

Children have the opportunity to:

- Ask for help when needed.
- Persevere when learning a new technique.
- Work cooperatively with others.

Areas of Learning: Literacy

Children have the opportunity to:

- Record the patterns they have made.
- Write instructions.

Areas of Learning: Mathematics

Children have the opportunity to:

- Create and comment on patterns and shapes.
- Record the length of time it takes them to weave one piece of material.

Areas of Learning: Understanding the World

Children have the opportunity to:

- Show an interest in how things are made.

Areas of Learning: Expressive Arts and Design

Children have the opportunity to:

- Learn new techniques.
- Make and explore patterns.

Being involved and concentrating

Questions for the children:

- Can you make a repeating pattern?

- How many pieces of material can you weave before the sand timer runs out?

- Could you give instructions to someone else to explain how to weave?

 "I can get in through 6 rectangles in the fence."

 "It's like decorating."

How does the activity enable children to develop and demonstrate the characteristics of effective learning?

Characteristic of effective learning	The enabling environment: Weaving
Playing and exploring – engagement ● Finding out and exploring. ● Playing with what they know. ● Being willing to 'have a go'.	Children can see an end goal that they want to achieve.
Active learning – motivation ● Being involved and concentrating. ● Keeping trying. ● Enjoying achieving what they set out to do.	The activity requires high levels of concentration and focus. Children can persevere.
Creating and thinking critically – thinking ● Having their own ideas. ● Making links. ● Choosing ways to do things.	Children can work out the best way of achieving an end goal through, adapting technique where they need to.

Working out the best way to keep hold of the material

From lavender and mint to 'eau de toilette'

Making perfume

Setting up the provision

Method

Set up a tray of shallow water and an assortment of mixing resources and scissors next to the herbs. Add science goggles for added appeal.

Resources

- Scented plants, herbs and colourful flowers
- Test tubes and pots
- Science lab goggles
- Funnels
- Sieves
- Scissors
- Scoops
- Pipettes and syringes (always without needles)
- Recycled spray bottles
- Clipboards and pens.

Handy hints

- Support children to carefully take cuttings of leaves and flowers to be used in their perfume. Ensure children are aware that this is an adult led activity and that they should not be cutting flowers at any other time. (Important if you want to preserve your plants!)

- Once children have taken their cuttings, they can be encouraged to work more independently. Selecting the resources that they think will best suit their objective.

Questions to help you extend the activity and to ensure challenge

Questions for you:

- Are there opportunities for children to list the ingredients in their perfume?

- Is there key vocabulary for the activity displayed?

How does the activity enable children to develop and demonstrate the characteristics of effective learning?

Characteristic of effective learning	The enabling environment: Making perfume
Playing and exploring – engagement ● Finding out and exploring. ● Playing with what they know. ● Being willing to 'have a go'.	The activity is multi-sensory. Children can use familiar objects in new ways. Children can engage in role play.
Active learning – motivation ● Being involved and concentrating. ● Keeping trying. ● Enjoying achieving what they set out to do.	Children can persevere when using tools and new techniques.
Creating and thinking critically – thinking ● Having their own ideas. ● Making links. ● Choosing ways to do things.	Children can adapt their work to suit their preferences.

Cutting some lavender to add to her perfume

How the activity can support children's development across the 7 areas of learning

Areas of Learning: Communication and Language

Children have the opportunity to:
- Describe the changing smells and textures.

Areas of Learning: Physical Development

Children have the opportunity to:
- Develop their skills using scissors and other one handed tools such as pipettes and tweezers.
- Develop an awareness of safety when using tools.

Areas of Learning: Personal, Social and Emotional Development

Children have the opportunity to:
- Express their own opinions.
- Talk about what they like and don't like.

Areas of Learning: Literacy

Children have the opportunity to:
- To write lists and instructions.
- To draw and label.

Areas of Learning: Mathematics

Children have the opportunity to:
- Explore capacity and weight.

Areas of Learning: Understanding the World

Children have the opportunity to:
- Comment on cause and effect.
- Use tools for a specific purpose

Areas of Learning: Expressive Arts and Design

Children have the opportunity to:
- Develop new techniques.
- Describe texture and smell.

Questions for the children:
- How could you describe the smell of your perfume?
- What did you find difficult about making your perfume?
- What tools could you use to remove the leaves and petals from your perfume?

"We need to mix the lavender in the water to make the smell come out."

"You have to squeeze it for the water to get in. You can make little drops with it."

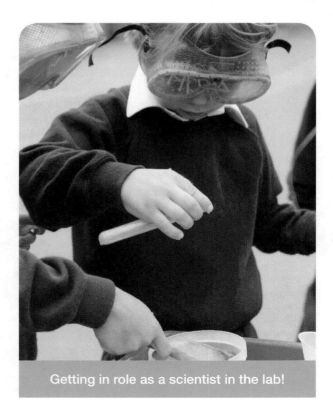
Getting in role as a scientist in the lab!

Shaving foam or delicious butter cream icing?

Shaving foam cakes

Targeted areas of learning:
Physical Development and
Expressive Arts and Design

> "If you squeeze the icing
> out of the cake, it explodes!"

Setting up the provision

Method

Arrange cake cases, some already filled with foam, on
a tray. Decorate the tray with coloured sand, glitter and
gems. Leave the foam available for children to top up
their cakes. Add different tools to allow children to find
the best way of filling up their cake cases.

Resources

- Cupcake cases
- Scoops
- Shaving foam
- Glitter
- Gem stones
- Colored sand.

Handy hints

- Silicone cake cases are easy to wash and can be
  reused again and again.

- A sprinkling of coloured sand on the tray means that
  children can collect a pinch to decorate their cakes.

- Swap the cake cases for bowls and spoons and you
  have an ice cream factory.

Questions to help you extend the activity and to ensure challenge

Questions for you:

- Are children able to self-select and add new resources
  to the activity?

How the activity can support children's development across the 7 areas of learning

Areas of Learning: Communication and Language
Children have the opportunity to:
- Describe the appearance, texture and smell of the resources.
- Talk about their own experiences of baking, birthdays etc.

Areas of Learning: Physical Development
Children have the opportunity to:
- Manipulate materials to achieve a planned effect.

Areas of Learning: Personal, Social and Emotional Development
Children have the opportunity to:
- Share resources.
- Share ideas.
- Seek delight in new experiences.

Areas of Learning: Literacy
Children have the opportunity to:
- Write and mark make in the foam.

Areas of Learning: Mathematics
Children have the opportunity to:
- Share cakes and toppings equally.
- Count decorations.
- Explore capacity.

Areas of Learning: Understanding the World
Children have the opportunity to:
- Talk about their own experiences of baking, birthdays etc.

Areas of Learning: Expressive Arts and Design
Children have the opportunity to:
- Engage in role play.
- Explore and describe the texture, smell and appearance of their cakes.

Working out the best way to fill up the cake cases

- Are there recipe books or recipe cards available?

Questions for the children:
- Can you share the cake cases out equally between the three of you?

- Which cake has the most decorations on it?

- How many different ways can you get the cake mixture into the cases?

 "I love the soft, slippery foam."

 "I have decorated 3 cakes. I have given each one three cherries so it's fair."

How does the activity enable children to develop and demonstrate the characteristics of effective learning?

Characteristic of effective learning	The enabling environment: Shaving foam cakes
Playing and exploring – engagement ● Finding out and exploring. ● Playing with what they know. ● Being willing to 'have a go'.	The activity is open-ended and multi-sensory. The scene and resources are relevant and familiar.
Active learning – motivation ● Being involved and concentrating. ● Keeping trying. ● Enjoying achieving what they set out to do.	Children will enjoy the appealing colours, textures and theme.
Creating and thinking critically – thinking ● Having their own ideas. ● Making links. ● Choosing ways to do things.	Children can decide how the resources are to be used.

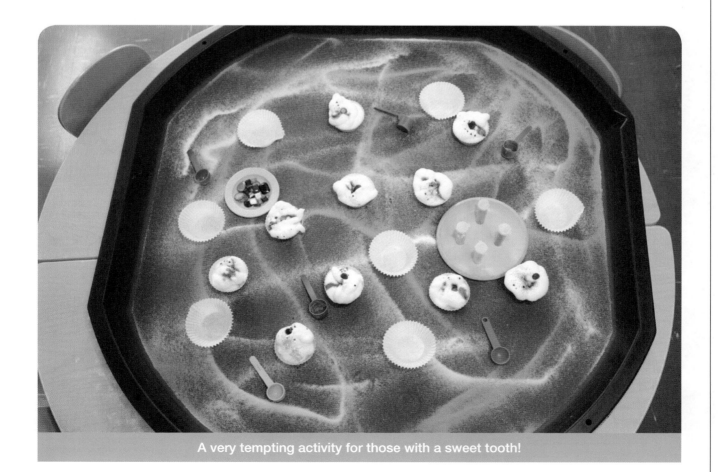

A very tempting activity for those with a sweet tooth!

An alien invasion thanks to just three simple ingredients

Slime

Setting up the provision

Method

Empty corn flour into a builder's tray. Spread across to cover the tray. Add water and food colouring, adjusting the quantity to achieve the consistency you want. Mix with your hands!

Resources

- Corn flour
- Food colouring
- Water
- Builder's tray
- Pipettes
- Small containers of different coloured paint mixed with water.

Handy hints

- Leave small containers of different coloured water at one end of the tray for children to dip into with their pipettes and then add to the corn flour.

- If you keep the mixture moving quickly in your hands it will become a solid, as soon as you stop the mixture moving it becomes a liquid.

- Set the activity up with the children so that they can see what happens as the different ingredients combine.

Questions to help you extend the activity and to ensure challenge

Questions for you

- Where else around the setting could you leave clues of an alien invasion?

- Can children continue to explore color mixing at other activities in the environment?

How does the activity enable children to develop and demonstrate the characteristics of effective learning?

Characteristic of effective learning	The enabling environment: Slime
Playing and exploring – engagement ● Finding out and exploring. ● Playing with what they know. ● Being willing to 'have a go'.	The activity is open-ended and multi-sensory. The appearance of the activity will draw children to try it out and 'have a go'. The unusual activity will cause intrigue and fascination.
Active learning – motivation ● Being involved and concentrating. ● Keeping trying. ● Enjoying achieving what they set out to do.	Children can show high levels of energy and fascination, playing close attention to detail as the corn flour and water continually changes.
Creating and thinking critically – thinking ● Having their own ideas. ● Making links. ● Choosing ways to do things.	Children can make predictions about what will happen when different colours are mixed together and how different ingredients will react with each other.

Ready to investigate how the coloured water will react with the corn flour

How the activity can support children's development across the 7 areas of learning

Areas of Learning: Communication and Language
Children have the opportunity to:
- Describe appearance and texture.
- Comment on the way the ingredients react with each other.

Areas of Learning: Physical Development
Children have the opportunity to:
- Handle small tools such as pipettes.

Areas of Learning: Personal, Social and Emotional Development
Children have the opportunity to:
- Take a risk, getting messy and exploring new materials.

Areas of Learning: Literacy
Children have the opportunity to:
- Use the shallow slime to write in, using their fingers or the end of paintbrushes.

Areas of Learning: Mathematics
Children have the opportunity to:
- Measure the quantities of the ingredients.
- Comment on the shapes and patterns made by the food colouring.

Areas of Learning: Understanding the World
Children have the opportunity to:
- Comment on the way the ingredients react with each other.

Areas of Learning: Expressive Arts and Design
Children have the opportunity to:
- Use their senses to comment on appearance and texture.

- How could you use the slime as inspiration for a story writing focus?

Questions for the children
- Is the slime a solid or a liquid? Can you find a way to make both?
- How could you describe how the slime moves through your fingers?
- What creature do you think would have slime like this?

"It's dripping and slipping when I scoop it up."

"I think it's going to turn me into a monster alien! "

Describing how the slime moves through his fingers and how it feels on his skin

Bring the scene to life!

Chapter Three: Small world

Key Areas of EYFS developed in this chapter:

- Expressive Arts and Design

- Communication and Language

- Literacy

- Understanding the World.

Activities for this chapter are:

- Jurassic adventures

- Desert life
- Down in the jungle
- The swamp
- Journey to Space
- At the beach
- Fairy garden.

Useful resources for activities in this chapter:

- Builder's tray
- Assorted size rocks, stones and logs
- Plants and leaves
- Story books
- Coloured sand
- Coloured paint
- Glitter.

Further provision ideas for this area:

- Under the sea
- African watering hole
- Gardens for the different seasons
- The moon
- Planet Mars
- Pond life
- Farmyard.

You will find specific links and resources for each activity in this chapter.

Realistic and dramatic small world scenes will create a language rich environment where children are inspired to become story tellers, actors and reporters.

Real examples of learning include:

"Let's see if we can dig for some real insects for the animals to eat for their lunch."

"We are putting all the bugs under the rock to keep them cool from the sun."

"We need to get the astronauts away from the sun so they don't burn."

Imagine you are really there and create a sense of drama

Observing dinosaurs in their natural environment is the only way to develop a paleontologist!

Jurassic adventures

Targeted areas of learning:
Communication and Language,
Expressive Arts and Design and Literacy

 "My dinosaur won't eat yours because he only eats plants."

Setting up the provision

Method
Arrange large dinosaurs amongst the plants, trees and bushes. Position leaves into the mouths of some dinosaurs to bring the scene to life.

Resources
- Bushes or a collection of plants.
- Fossils or interesting rocks and stones
- Logs
- Dinosaur storybooks and information books.

Handy hints
- The more overgrown the better when it comes to growing your setting

- Filming children as they act out stories with the props can provide entertaining viewing for everyone, including parents.

- Hide some large spherical stones amongst the plants as dinosaur eggs.

Questions to help you extend the activity and to ensure challenge

Questions for you
- Are there non-fiction books to hand?

- Are there dinosaur storybooks to hand?

- Are there props to enable children to get into character

How the activity can support children's development across the 7 areas of learning

Areas of Learning: Communication and Language
Children have the opportunity to:
- Develop a narrative to go alongside their play.
- Describe the setting.

Areas of Learning: Physical Development
Children have the opportunity to:
- Handle and manoeuvre larger resources.

Areas of Learning: Personal, Social and Emotional Development
Children have the opportunity to:
- Play alongside others engaged in the same theme.
- Work together to act out a narrative.

Areas of Learning: Literacy
Children have the opportunity to:
- Read non-fiction books.
- Write their own stories.

Areas of Learning: Mathematics
Children have the opportunity to:
- Comment and compare size and weight.

Areas of Learning: Understanding the World
Children have the opportunity to:
- Discuss and describe different habitats.
- Talk about past events.

Areas of Learning: Expressive Arts and Design
Children have the opportunity to:
- Engage in role play.

Discussing the diets of the different dinosaurs

as paleontologists? For example, tools, explorer hats, clipboards, notebooks.

Questions for the children
- Can you find each dinosaur in the information book?

- Can you make a map explaining how to get to Jurassic adventures?

"Let's draw all the big scary ones."

"Let's dig for Dinosaur bones like. We might find sharp teeth."

How does the activity enable children to develop and demonstrate the characteristics of effective learning?

Characteristic of effective learning	The enabling environment: Jurassic adventures
Playing and exploring – engagement ● Finding out and exploring. ● Playing with what they know. ● Being willing to 'have a go'.	The activity is open-ended and multi-sensory. Children can engage in imaginative play, getting in character as palaeontologists, or the dinosaurs themselves.
Active learning – motivation ● Being involved and concentrating. ● Keeping trying. ● Enjoying achieving what they set out to do.	The natural resources are unusual and intriguing, enabling children to show high levels of fascination and maintain sustained concentration as they explore.
Creating and thinking critically – thinking ● Having their own ideas. ● Making links. ● Choosing ways to do things.	Children have opportunities to talk about and explain their knowledge whilst developing their own ideas for storytelling and drama.

Ensuring the dinosaur has enough to eat!

A sprinkle of coloured sand turns a garden of harmless insects into a scorching desert rife with poisonous creatures

Desert life

Targeted areas of learning:
Communication and Language,
Expressive Arts and Design and Literacy

Setting up the provision

Method

Arrange plastic minibeasts and natural resources such as logs and stones onto a builder's tray. Create patterns and images as you pour the coloured sand over the tray to enhance the visual impact of the provision. Use yellow sand to create the sun for example or red sand to create a poisonous trail.

Resources

- Coloured sand – warm colours
- Stones, rocks and logs
- Plastic minibeasts
- Non-fiction books
- Magnifying glasses.

Handy hints

- Swapping the sand for a handful of grass and leaves takes you back to a quiet English garden.

- Using sand in shakers allows you to create patterns and scenes.

- Allow children to match and sort the insects by including some insects that are identical or that differ only by their pattern.

Questions to help you extend the activity and to ensure challenge

Questions for you

- Are there opportunities to write stories, inspired by the resources?

- Are there opportunities for children to record the number of insects that are the same or different? Perhaps using tally charts or venn diagrams. Are there opportunities for children to analyse this data?

How does the activity enable children to develop and demonstrate the characteristics of effective learning?

Characteristic of effective learning	The enabling environment: Desert life
Playing and exploring – engagement ● Finding out and exploring. ● Playing with what they know. ● Being willing to 'have a go'.	The activity is open-ended. The vibrant colours mean the activity is eye-catching, and appealing.
Active learning – motivation ● Being involved and concentrating. ● Keeping trying. ● Enjoying achieving what they set out to do.	Through constant dialogue and questioning, children can develop their knowledge of the world and living things.
Creating and thinking critically – thinking ● Having their own ideas. ● Making links. ● Choosing ways to do things.	Children can explain their own knowledge and thoughts and listen to the ideas of others. They can make links using what they already know about these creatures.

Feel the heat from the coloured sand

How the activity can support children's development across the 7 areas of learning

Areas of Learning: Communication and Language

Children have the opportunity to:
- Describe the scene.
- Develop their vocabulary.

Areas of Learning: Physical Development

Children have the opportunity to:
- Develop control when handling small objects.

Areas of Learning: Personal, Social and Emotional Development

Children have the opportunity to:
- Take into consideration the ideas of others.
- Maintain focus for a sustained period of time

Areas of Learning: Literacy

Children have the opportunity to:
- Label drawings.
- Write stories.
- Write in the shallow sand.

Areas of Learning: Mathematics

Children have the opportunity to:
- Sort the minibeasts in various ways.

Areas of Learning: Understanding the World

Children have the opportunity to:
- Discuss and describe different habitats.
- Discuss and describe different weather types.

Areas of Learning: Expressive Arts and Design

Children have the opportunity to:
- Comment on and describe the colours and patterns created by the sand.

Questions for the children
- How could you sort the insects?

- Where in the world could this desert be?

 "I am drawing all the bugs I can see and their names."

 "We are putting all the bugs under the rock to keep them cool from the sun."

"Do you think it is a desert in Egypt?"

Writing a list of poisonous bugs on one side of the paper and harmless bugs on the other side

Adults may see a collection of plants; children will see a mysterious land inviting adventure

Down in the jungle

Targeted areas of learning:
Communication and Language,
Expressive Arts and Design and Literacy

Setting up the provision

Method

Create a jungle scene amongst the plants outside by positioning the animals so that they are basking in the sun or resting in the shade.

Resources

- Plants and bushes outside
- Plastic jungle animals
- Colourful fabric
- Binoculars.

Handy hints

- Only real plants and real light can create the sun and shade needed for these animals.

"Let's make sure the baby animals are all under the shade to keep cool."

"Let's see if we can dig for some real insects for the animals to eat for their lunch."

Questions to help you extend the activity and to ensure challenge

Questions for you

- Are there props to support explorers role play?

- Could you add instruments nearby to create the sounds of the jungle? Could you record these sounds for children to listen and respond to?

How the activity can support children's development across the 7 areas of learning

Areas of Learning: Communication and Language

Children have the opportunity to:

- Develop a narrative to go alongside their play.
- Describe the setting.

Areas of Learning: Physical Development

Children have the opportunity to:

- Handle and manoeuvre larger resources.

Areas of Learning: Personal, Social and Emotional Development

Children have the opportunity to:

- Play alongside others engaged in the same theme.
- Work together to act out a narrative.

Areas of Learning: Literacy

Children have the opportunity to:

- Read non-fiction books.
- Write their own stories.

Areas of Learning: Mathematics

Children have the opportunity to:

- Comment and compare size and weight.

Areas of Learning: Understanding the World

Children have the opportunity to:

- Discuss and describe different habitats.
- Discuss their own experiences of seeing these animals.

Areas of Learning: Expressive Arts and Design

Children have the opportunity to:

- Engage in role play.
- Make up and sing familiar songs.

Seeking shade from the midday sun. Using plants outside helps to create a more realistic scene

 "The giraffes like to eat the big leaves from these plants, they can reach right up to the tall ones."

Questions for the children

- Which animal do you think would be the king of this jungle?

- Where in the world do you think this jungle is?

- Can you sing any songs about jungle animals?

How does the activity enable children to develop and demonstrate the characteristics of effective learning?

Characteristic of effective learning	The enabling environment: Down in the jungle
Playing and exploring – engagement • Finding out and exploring. • Playing with what they know. • Being willing to 'have a go'.	The activity is open-ended and multi-sensory. Children represent experiences through imaginative play, getting in character as explorers, or as the animals themselves.
Active learning – motivation • Being involved and concentrating. • Keeping trying. • Enjoying achieving what they set out to do.	The natural resources are intriguing, enabling children to show high levels of fascination and maintain sustained concentration as they explore.
Creating and thinking critically – thinking • Having their own ideas. • Making links. • Choosing ways to do things.	Children can use the plants and animals to continually change the scene and the atmosphere. For example, a relaxing morning at the watering hole may turn into a ferocious hunt in the midday sun.

A battle between child and snake ensues…!

A trip to space isn't that far when you have black paint and silver foil to hand!

Journey to Space

Setting up the provision

Method

Mix black paint in the water tray until it is jet black.
Add glitter, foil and assorted sized spheres. Create
rockets using whatever you have to hand. For example,
junk modelling resources such as plastic tubs or yoghurt
pots. Add play people as your astronauts.

Resources

- Black paint
- Assorted size and colour balls
- Play people
- Silver foil
- Glitter
- Rocks.

Handy hints

- Drape dark material above or to the side of the water
  tray to enhance the space scene

- Staple key vocabulary to this material

- Leave a roll of foil by the tray for children to create their
  own moon rocks and asteroids.

Questions to help you extend the activity and to ensure challenge

Questions for you

- Are there information books nearby?

- Are the key questions and vocabulary hanging
  near the water tray?

Questions for the children

- Can you order the planets by size?

- Can you name any of the planets?

How does the activity enable children to develop and demonstrate the characteristics of effective learning?

Characteristic of effective learning	The enabling environment: Journey to Space
Playing and exploring – engagement ● Finding out and exploring. ● Playing with what they know. ● Being willing to 'have a go'.	The activity is open-ended and multi-sensory. Children can engage in imaginative play, getting in character as astronauts.
Active learning – motivation ● Being involved and concentrating. ● Keeping trying. ● Enjoying achieving what they set out to do.	Children can immerse themselves in storytelling and drama, maintaining their focus for a sustained period of time.
Creating and thinking critically – thinking ● Having their own ideas. ● Making links. ● Choosing ways to do things.	Children have opportunities to talk about and explain their own knowledge and use information books to develop this further. They can make their own decision about how resources are to be used. For example, what do the spheres represent? How can the foil be used?

The Solar System awaits the young astronomer!

How the activity can support children's development across the 7 areas of learning

Areas of Learning: Communication and Language
Children have the opportunity to:
- Develop a narrative to go alongside their play.
- Develop their vocabulary.

Areas of Learning: Physical Development
Children have the opportunity to:
- Manipulate materials to achieved a planned effect – using the foil.

Areas of Learning: Personal, Social and Emotional Development
Children have the opportunity to:
- Play alongside other children engaged in the same them.
- Share resources.

Areas of Learning: Literacy
Children have the opportunity to:
- Read key vocabulary related to the topic.
- Read non-fiction books elsewhere in the environment.

Areas of Learning: Mathematics
Children have the opportunity to:
- Order planets by size.
- Sort planets and other objects by colour.
- Explore floating and sinking.

Areas of Learning: Understanding the World
Children have the opportunity to:
- Show an interest in other professions.
- Show curiosity out about the world.

Areas of Learning: Expressive Arts and Design
Children have the opportunity to:
- Engage in role play.

- Can you use the foil to make space suits for the astronauts?

- Can you write some safety instructions for the astronauts?

 "We will land on Mars in 9 minutes."

"It is so dark, let's collect all the glittery stars."

"We need to get the astronauts away from the sun so they don't burn."

Naming the planets as they move around the sun

A splash of green paint and a handful of mud transforms the water tray into a boggy swamp

The swamp

Targeted areas of learning:
Communication and Language,
Expressive Arts and Design

**"He is drinking the slime that
is coming out of the leaves."**

Setting up the provision

Method

Mix green water in the water tray. Add a couple of handful of soils to one corner and create a barrier around it with stones and logs. Add a selection of plants or green leaves, carefully positioned so that they are growing up out of the swamp.

Resources

- A selection of plastic creatures
- Water
- Green paint
- Soils
- Grass
- Plant cuttings
- Logs and stone.

Handy hints

- Who lives in the swamp? Let the children decide.

- Put in some green jelly to add a different texture.

- As you make the jelly, place a couple of animals inside the mould so that they set inside the mixture.

Questions to help you extend the activity and to ensure challenge

Questions for you:

- Have children helped to create the swamp?

- Have you included real life materials such as plants from outside?

How the activity can support children's development across the 7 areas of learning

Areas of Learning: Communication and Language

Children have the opportunity to:

- Develop a narrative to go alongside their play.
- Describe the setting.

Areas of Learning: Physical Development

Children have the opportunity to:

- Handle and manoeuvre both small and larger resources.

Areas of Learning: Personal, Social and Emotional Development

Children have the opportunity to:

- Play alongside other children engaged in the same theme.
- Work together to act out a narrative.
- Make decisions about what resources should be used.

Areas of Learning: Literacy

Children have the opportunity to:

- Write swamp stories.
- Create and develop their own characters as they play.

Areas of Learning: Mathematics

Children have the opportunity to:

- Explore floating and sinking.

Areas of Learning: Understanding the World

Children have the opportunity to:

- Discuss and describe different habitats.
- Describe and identify different plants.

Areas of Learning: Expressive Arts and Design

Children have the opportunity to:

- Engage in role play.

Finding nutrients for the dinosaurs in the murky swamp water

Questions for the children:

- Who lives in your swamp?

- What is a swamp?

- Can you draw and label a picture of this swamp?

"I think it's a hot swamp, can we put some warm water in?"

"Pigs and toads would like it in here too."

How does the activity enable children to develop and demonstrate the characteristics of effective learning?

Characteristic of effective learning	The enabling environment: The swamp
Playing and exploring – engagement ● Finding out and exploring. ● Playing with what they know. ● Being willing to 'have a go'.	The activity is open-ended and multi-sensory. Children can engage in imaginative play, developing their own narratives.
Active learning – motivation ● Being involved and concentrating. ● Keeping trying. ● Enjoying achieving what they set out to do.	Children can immerse themselves in storytelling and drama, maintaining their focus for a sustained period of time.
Creating and thinking critically – thinking ● Having their own ideas. ● Making links. ● Choosing ways to do things.	Children can decide and select which animals should live in the swamp and why?

Prehistoric plants emerge from the shallow water

A holiday by the sea has never been closer

At the beach

Targeted areas of learning:
Communication and Language
and Expressive Arts and Design

Setting up the provision

Method

Pour sand onto one half of the tray and water onto the other half, creating a barrier with shells and stones. Add blue paint to the water. Position shells, sea creatures and play people to complete the scene.

Resources

- Sand
- Blue paint
- Boats
- Play people
- Plastic sea creatures
- Assorted size shells
- Pebbles.

Handy hints

- Create a barrier between the sand and water, with the pebbles and shells, to stop the water from running.

- Colour the water with blue paint to make the scene more vibrant.

Questions to help you extend the activity and to ensure challenge

Questions for you:

- Have the children been able to help set the scene, drawing on their own experiences to decide what is needed?

- Are there books about journeys and holidays available elsewhere in the environment?

Questions for the children

- Which creatures can live on the land and in the sea?

- Where in the world could this beach be?

How does the activity enable children to develop and demonstrate the characteristics of effective learning?

Characteristic of effective learning	The enabling environment: At the beach
Playing and exploring – engagement • Finding out and exploring. • Playing with what they know. • Being willing to 'have a go'.	The activity is open-ended and multi-sensory. Children can represent their own experiences through their play.
Active learning – motivation • Being involved and concentrating. • Keeping trying. • Enjoying achieving what they set out to do.	Children can immerse themselves in storytelling and drama, maintaining their focus for a sustained period of time.
Creating and thinking critically – thinking • Having their own ideas. • Making links. • Choosing ways to do things.	As children help set up the scene, they can decide how to separate the sand and water using trial and error. They can decide where different objects should be placed based on their own knowledge and experiences.

A setting fit for the greatest of adventures

How the activity can support children's development across the 7 areas of learning

Areas of Learning: Communication and Language

Children have the opportunity to:

- Develop a narrative to go alongside their play.
- Describe the setting.

Areas of Learning: Physical Development

Children have the opportunity to:

- Develop control when handling smaller resources.

Areas of Learning: Personal, Social and Emotional Development

Children have the opportunity to:

- Play alongside others engaged in the same theme.
- Work together to act out a narrative.
- Make decisions about what resources should be used.

Areas of Learning: Literacy

Children have the opportunity to:

- Read stories about journeys and holidays.
- Write stories about journeys, holidays and past experiences.

Areas of Learning: Mathematics

Children have the opportunity to:

- Describe the size and shape of the shells.
- Explore objects that float and sink.

Areas of Learning: Understanding the World

Children have the opportunity to:

- Discuss different weather types.
- Show an interest in other countries.
- Talk about personal experiences.

Areas of Learning: Expressive Arts and Design

Children have the opportunity to:

- Engage in role play.

  "The giant shell is for the monster snail that lives at this beach."

  "Oh no! The tide is coming in, everyone is being washed away."

"We had to get a bus, a train and an aeroplane here."

 "When I put the stones in the water they sink."

Attack of the giant squid! Absorbed in storytelling

Where will the fairy dust take you?

Fairy garden

Targeted areas of learning:
Communication and Language,
Expressive Arts and Design and Literacy

"Can you hear the sea in the shell? That's where you will end up if you climb inside."

Setting up the provision

Method

Arrange a selection of ponies or creatures of your choice to create a fairytale scene amongst a growing area outside. Sprinkle glitter on the leaves and petals and scatter colourful feathers all around.

Resources

- Plants, flowers, any growing area
- Coloured feathers
- Shells
- Plastic gems
- Glitter
- Ponies, unicorns, butterflies and any other fairytale creatures you may have.

Handy hints

- Bury gems under the soil and mark where children should dig by sprinkling glitter into the shape of an X.

- Have fancy dress clothes available for children to completely immerse themselves in their adventure. Wings and capes often prove very popular.

Questions to help you extend the activity and to ensure challenge

Questions for you:

- Are there fairy stories available to support role play?

- Are there notebooks and pens for children to write lists, stories, clues etc?

How the activity can support children's development across the 7 areas of learning

Areas of Learning: Communication and Language

Children have the opportunity to:

- Develop a narrative to go alongside their play.
- Describe the setting.

Areas of Learning: Physical Development

Children have the opportunity to:

- Handle and manoeuvre larger resources.

Areas of Learning: Personal, Social and Emotional Development

Children have the opportunity to:

- Play alongside others engaged in the same theme.
- Work together to act out a narrative.

Areas of Learning: Literacy

Children have the opportunity to:

- Read non-fiction books.
- Write their own stories.

Areas of Learning: Mathematics

Children have the opportunity to:

- Make maps of the fairy garden.

Areas of Learning: Understanding the World

Children have the opportunity to:

- Discuss and describe different habitats.
- Talk about past events.

Areas of Learning: Expressive Arts and Design

Children have the opportunity to:

- Engage in role play.

This is certainly not just a place for girls!

- Are there craft resources for children to make props to support their play?

Questions for the children:

- What fairytale stories do you know?

- Can you draw and design your own fairytale land?

 "The ponies are on an adventure to save the Princess from the Witch."

 "If we sprinkle the fairy dust on the plants they will turn into sweets."

How does the activity enable children to develop and demonstrate the characteristics of effective learning?

Characteristic of effective learning	The enabling environment: Fairy garden
Playing and exploring – engagement ● Finding out and exploring. ● Playing with what they know. ● Being willing to 'have a go'.	The activity is open-ended and multi-sensory. Children can engage in imaginative play, drawing on influences from adventure stories and fairy tales.
Active learning – motivation ● Being involved and concentrating. ● Keeping trying. ● Enjoying achieving what they set out to do.	Children can immerse themselves in storytelling and drama, maintaining their focus for a sustained period of time.
Creating and thinking critically – thinking ● Having their own ideas. ● Making links. ● Choosing ways to do things.	Children can make their own decision about how resources are to be used and have the opportunity to add to the scene with objects that thy think would enhance it.

A magical activity to inspire role play and storytelling

Paint and pens are great, but what else could you use to inspire a master piece?

Chapter Four: Creativity

Key areas of EYFS developed in this chapter:

- Expressive Arts and Design

- Physical Development

- Understanding the World

- Literacy.

Activities for this chapter are:

- Music wall
- Making faces
- Swirl and mix
- Cave writing
- Spaghetti art
- Bubbles
- Symmetry.

Useful resources for activities in this chapter:

- Assorted writing and painting tools
- Coloured paint
- Washing up liquid
- Food colouring
- Shaving foam.

Further provision ideas for this area:

- Lava lamps – mixing oil, glitter and coloured water
- Painting with tea bags
- Painting on old wall paper
- Still life drawings

- Colour mixing with paint and straws
- Workshop area
- Melting old crayons into silicone moulds to make new multi coloured crayons.

You will find specific links and resources for each activity in this chapter.

Using the same resources in different ways can create whole new experiences. When time is so valuable being resourceful in this way allows you to be creative without compromising the quality of the provision.

Real examples of learning include:

 "The bubbles are all sparkly. You can see different rainbow colours in them."

 "The wind is making the instruments play without us helping!"

"These leaves came from the tree in the playground. They fell off because it is winter."

How you present the activities is so important

More creative ways to utilise the fence

Music wall

Setting up the provision

Method
Attach assorted materials and instruments at different heights along a fence. Ensure there are a mixture of colours and textures.

Resources
- Spoons
- Chimes
- Foil plates
- A selection of percussion instruments
- Wooden sticks
- Tissue paper
- Pots and pans
- Bells.

Handy hints
- Make sure the instruments can be reached by everyone

- Include a mix of real instruments and everyday objects to stimulate conversation and comparisons

- Having the wall outside means that the children can be as loud as they want!

Questions to help you extend the activity and to ensure challenge

Questions for you:
- Are there familiar song lyrics displayed?

- Are there pictures of characters from familiar songs displayed?

- Are there opportunities to film the children in action?

- Are there opportunities for children to write down the lyrics of new songs they make up?

How does the activity enable children to develop and demonstrate the characteristics of effective learning?

Characteristic of effective learning	The enabling environment: Music wall
Playing and exploring – engagement ● Finding out and exploring. ● Playing with what they know. ● Being willing to 'have a go'.	Children can explore the instruments in whatever way they choose. For example, banging, shaking, tapping. There is a mixture of familiar instruments and new intriguing objects to be investigated.
Active learning – motivation ● Being involved and concentrating. ● Keeping trying. ● Enjoying achieving what they set out to do.	Children can maintain their focus as they sing along to familiar songs and rhymes.
Creating and thinking critically – thinking ● Having their own ideas. ● Making links. ● Choosing ways to do things.	Children can decide how the instruments can be played, expressing the own opinions on the sounds created. The activity enables children to explore new ways to create and change sounds. Children can make links between music and emotions.

Trying to find the instrument that will make the loudest sound

How the activity can support children's development across the 7 areas of learning

Areas of Learning: Communication and Language
Children have the opportunity to:
- Develop their vocabulary, learning the names of new instruments.
- Describe the sounds they can hear.

Areas of Learning: Physical Development
Children have the opportunity to:
- Develop control over objects to achieve a planned outcome.

Areas of Learning: Personal, Social and Emotional Development
Children have the opportunity to:
- Take into consideration other children's ideas.
- Develop the confidence to try new activities.
- Work with other children to create music.

Areas of Learning: Literacy
Children have the opportunity to:
- Draw and label the instruments.

Areas of Learning: Mathematics
Children have the opportunity to:
- Describe the shape and size of the instruments.

Areas of Learning: Understanding the World
Children have the opportunity to:
- Use their senses to explore new materials.
- Develop their understanding of cause and effect by recognising and explaining how the sounds are being produced.

Areas of Learning: Expressive Arts and Design
Children have the opportunity to:
- Create simple rhythms.
- Dance.
- Explore how to make quiet and loud sounds.
- Build up a repertoire of songs and rhymes.
- Make up their own songs and rhymes.
- Describe different sounds.

Questions for the children:
- Can you make a loud sound? Can you make a quiet sound?
- What other objects could we turn into instruments to add to our musical wall?

"Let's make it as loud as we can."

"Do you want to come and dance to our music?"

"The wind is making the instruments play without us helping!"

Create different levels, textures, colours and shapes on the fence

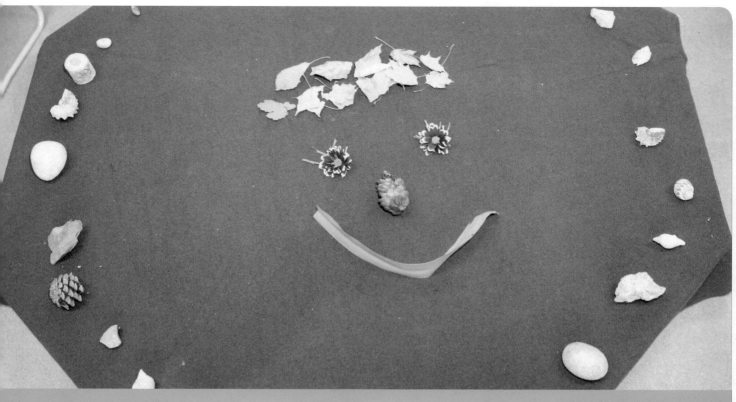

Petals and leaves or eyes and hair? What do you see?

Making faces

Targeted areas of learning:
Expressive Arts and Design
and Understanding the World

 "I need to use the small
leaves for the hair and
the big leaves for the ears."

Setting up the provision

Method
Arrange the natural materials into pictures or patterns to
model how the resources can be used creatively.

Resources
- Stones
- Shells
- Assorted colour and shape leaves
- Fir cones
- Petals.

Handy hints
- Go on a local walk so that children can collect the
  materials for the activity themselves.

- Invite children to bring in objects from home that could
  contribute to the activity. For example, shells from a
  trip to the beach or sticks from the park.

- Children can use the resources to make their own
  story settings.

Questions to help you extend the activity and to ensure challenge

Questions for you:
- Are there opportunities for children to plan what they
  will create beforehand?

- Are there opportunities to discuss what each of the
  objects are and where they have come from?

How the activity can support children's development across the 7 areas of learning

Areas of Learning: Communication and Language

Children have the opportunity to:
- Describe and comment on their patterns and pictures.
- Talk about what they are doing as they create.

Areas of Learning: Physical Development

Children have the opportunity to:
- Handle and arrange small objects.

Areas of Learning: Personal, Social and Emotional Development

Children have the opportunity to:
- Develop an inquisitive mind.
- Share resources.
- Work cooperatively with others.

Areas of Learning: Literacy

Children have the opportunity to:
- Create their own story settings.
- Write labels for the objects they have used.

Areas of Learning: Mathematics

Children have the opportunity to:
- Count and compare the number and size of the objects.

Areas of Learning: Understanding the World

Children have the opportunity to:
- Discuss growth, decay and changes over time.
- Explore the local environment.

Areas of Learning: Expressive Arts and Design

Children have the opportunity to:
- Make representations of objects, people. and events using a variety of resources.

Organising his carefully-chosen resources

Questions for the children:
- Can you make a picture using just 7 of the objects?

- Can you describe how you have made your picture?

> "These leaves came from the tree in the playground. They fell off because it is winter."

> "I have got seven sticks, I'm going to make arms and legs."

How does the activity enable children to develop and demonstrate the characteristics of effective learning?

Characteristic of effective learning	The enabling environment: Making faces
Playing and exploring – engagement ● Finding out and exploring. ● Playing with what they know. ● Being willing to 'have a go'.	The activity is open-ended and multi sensory. The materials will be familiar yet children can use them in new ways.
Active learning – motivation ● Being involved and concentrating. ● Keeping trying. ● Enjoying achieving what they set out to do.	Children can work with a purpose in mind and maintain focus until they have achieved their end goal.
Creating and thinking critically – thinking ● Having their own ideas. ● Making links. ● Choosing ways to do things.	Children can adapt their work and make choices about the objects they choose and how they are arranged.

Arranging the resources to create a picture of yourself

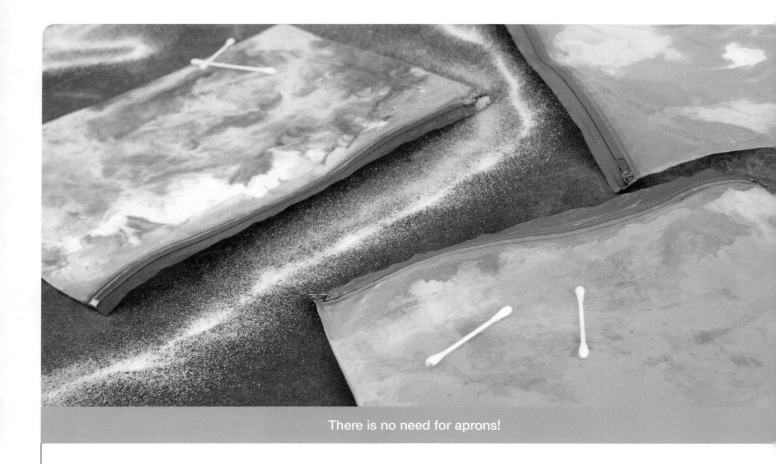

There is no need for aprons!

Mix and swirl

Targeted areas of learning:
Expressive Arts and Design
and Understanding the World

Setting up the provision

Method
Squeeze paint into zipper plastic wallet, ensuring that
the paint spreads across the sides of the bag rather than
falling straight to the bottom.

Resources
- Zipper plastic wallets
- Paint
- Cotton buds.

Handy hints
- If you don't have zipper plastic wallets, any plastic
  sleeve will work as long as you seal the top with tape.

- Plastic glue spatulas and the ends of paintbrushes
  provide another way to mix and mark make in the paint.

Questions to help you extend the activity and to ensure challenge

Questions for you:
- Are there letters and numbers displayed to encourage
  children to write these in the paint?

- Are there opportunities for children to create their own
  paint wallets?

Questions for the children:
- What can you write in the paint? Can you write your
  friend's name?

 "I can move the paint into a swirly pattern with my finger."

How does the activity enable children to develop and demonstrate the characteristics of effective learning?

Characteristic of effective learning	The enabling environment: Mix and swirl
Playing and exploring – engagement ● Finding out and exploring. ● Playing with what they know. ● Being willing to 'have a go'.	Children can explore new ways of using what is familiar to them. Children can find out what happens to the paint as they experiment with different tools and techniques.
Active learning – motivation ● Being involved and concentrating. ● Keeping trying. ● Enjoying achieving what they set out to do.	The use of the zip lock bag means that there is no need for mess on this occasion. The activity is therefore accessible to those children who would not normally engage with messy play.
Creating and thinking critically – thinking ● Having their own ideas. ● Making links. ● Choosing ways to do things.	Children can experiment with and decide which tools are the most effective. Children can explore colour mixing and have the opportunity to describe cause and effect.

What can you see in the paint?

How the activity can support children's development across the 7 areas of learning

Areas of Learning: Communication and Language

Children have the opportunity to:
- Answer 'how' and 'why' questions about their experiences.
- Describe what they are doing.

Areas of Learning: Physical Development

Children have the opportunity to:
- Develop control over tools for mark making.

Areas of Learning: Personal, Social and Emotional Development

Children have the opportunity to:
- Try new activities.
- Express their own ideas.

Areas of Learning: Literacy

Children have the opportunity to:
- Mark make and write in different materials.

Areas of Learning: Mathematics

Children have the opportunity to:
- Comment on and describe patterns and shapes.

Areas of Learning: Understanding the World

Children have the opportunity to:
- Explore what happens when colours are mixed.

Areas of Learning: Expressive Arts and Design

Children have the opportunity to:
- Experiment with pattern and colour in new ways, using new materials.

- Can you see any pictures in the paint?

- What colours can you make by mixing the paint together?

 "I can write numbers in the paint. Look it's a 2."

 "The colours can mix if you spread them together."

Trying to move the white paint from the top of the wallet to the bottom, using just her fingers

Inspire children's writing

Cave writing

Targeted areas of learning:
Expressive Arts and Design and Literacy

"I'm writing a secret message."

Setting up the provision

Method
Drape dark material over the table and cover the underside with large sheets of paper. Add a selection of writing tools.

Resources
- Table
- Dark material
- Large sheets of paper
- Writing tools
- Masking tape.

Handy hints
- Swap the writing tools for paints

- Add torches to add to the cave experience!

Questions to help you extend the activity and to ensure challenge

Questions for you:
- Could this activity be extended into a role play area?

- Is there a selection of different types of writing tools?

- What stories books could link with this activity?

Questions for the children:
- Can you write a message for a friend?

- Can you draw the animals that might live in this cave?

- What stories do you know that have a cave in them?

How the activity can support children's development across the 7 areas of learning

Areas of Learning: Communication and Language

Children have the opportunity to:
- Develop a narrative as they write and draw.

Areas of Learning: Physical Development

Children have the opportunity to:
- Develop control over writing tools.
- Develop spatial awareness.

Areas of Learning: Personal, Social and Emotional Development

Children have the opportunity to:
- Share the small space cooperatively with others.
- Take into account the ideas of others, deciding how to organise the activity.

Areas of Learning: Literacy

Children have the opportunity to:
- Write and mark make with a selection of tools.
- Ascribe meaning to their marks.
- Write for a purpose.
- Make links with books they know.

Areas of Learning: Mathematics

Children have the opportunity to:
- Draw shapes and patterns.
- Write numbers.
- Use positional language.

Areas of Learning: Understanding the World

Children have the opportunity to:
- Discuss different environments and how they vary.

Areas of Learning: Expressive Arts and Design

Children have the opportunity to:
- Draw and paint pictures.
- Engage in role play.

A perfect place for writing secret codes!

 "I have written a secret message can you read it?"

 "Let's write a story about the cave people and a dragon."

 "I'm drawing the sky."

  "This is so fun, I like lying down to draw."

How does the activity enable children to develop and demonstrate the characteristics of effective learning?

Characteristic of effective learning	The enabling environment: Cave writing
Playing and exploring – engagement ● Finding out and exploring. ● Playing with what they know. ● Being willing to 'have a go'.	The activity is open-ended. The resources are exciting, containing a balance of familiar and new experiences. Children can engage in imaginative play and develop narratives.
Active learning – motivation ● Being involved and concentrating. ● Keeping trying. ● Enjoying achieving what they set out to do.	The enclosed space is immediately inviting, allowing children to absorb themselves in the activity for a sustained period of time.
Creating and thinking critically – thinking ● Having their own ideas. ● Making links. ● Choosing ways to do things.	Children can decide what should be written or drawn and can develop the activity as they choose, sharing ideas with others.

Why write on a table when you can write underneath it?!

Spaghetti is not just for eating!

Spaghetti art

Setting up the provision

Method
Cook spaghetti and separate it into three bowls, mix a few drops of food colouring into each bowl to create three different colour choices.

Resources
- Spaghetti
- Food colouring
- Large paper
- Bowls.

Handy hints
- Support children to use the spaghetti to make a face with long hair. Children can then use scissors to trim the hair, acting as hairdressers!

- Model how to make different shapes by leaving an example spaghetti picture on display.

Questions to help you extend the activity and to ensure challenge

Questions for you:
- Could you leave high frequency words for children to try to make out of the spaghetti?

- Could you use a camera to take photos of children's work?

- Are their opportunities for children to plan and design their pictures first using pencils?

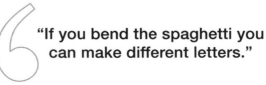

"If you bend the spaghetti you can make different letters."

How does the activity enable children to develop and demonstrate the characteristics of effective learning?

Characteristic of effective learning	The enabling environment: Spaghetti art
Playing and exploring – engagement ● Finding out and exploring. ● Playing with what they know. ● Being willing to 'have a go'.	The activity is open ended and multi-sensory. The appearance of the activity will draw children to try it out and 'have a go'. The opportunity to explore familiar foods in new ways is exciting and often amusing.
Active learning – motivation ● Being involved and concentrating. ● Keeping trying. ● Enjoying achieving what they set out to do.	Children can persevere to form letters, numbers and objects with the spaghetti. Children can maintain their focus to complete a picture.
Creating and thinking critically – thinking ● Having their own ideas. ● Making links. ● Choosing ways to do things.	Children can plan the picture they want to create and then choose how to manipulate materials to achieve this end goal.

Using careful precision to ensure the strands of spaghetti don't break

How the activity can support children's development across the 7 areas of learning

Areas of Learning: Communication and Language

Children have the opportunity to:
- Plan and describe what image they will create.
- Explain how they used the resources.

Areas of Learning: Physical Development

Children have the opportunity to:
- Develop a pincer grip as they handle and arrange the spaghetti.

Areas of Learning: Personal, Social and Emotional Development

Children have the opportunity to:
- Express their own ideas and opinions.
- Share resources with others.
- Work cooperatively with others to make a picture on a larger scale.

Areas of Learning: Literacy

Children have the opportunity to:
- Spell out familiar words.
- Form letters.

Areas of Learning: Mathematics

Children have the opportunity to:
- Make 2D shapes.
- Form numbers.
- Compare different lengths of spaghetti.

Areas of Learning: Understanding the World

Children have the opportunity to:
- Observe and comment on similarities, differences and change.
- Comment on the changing state of the spaghetti when mixed with boiling water.

Areas of Learning: Expressive Arts and Design

Children have the opportunity to:
- Use new materials for artistic purposes.
- Create representations of people and objects.
- Create patterns.

Questions for the children:
- Can you label your picture?
- Can you write your name using the spaghetti?
- What shapes have you created with the spaghetti?

 "I can make a rainbow with the different colours."

"I have squashed it together to make two eyes and a nose."

Delighted with her finished picture

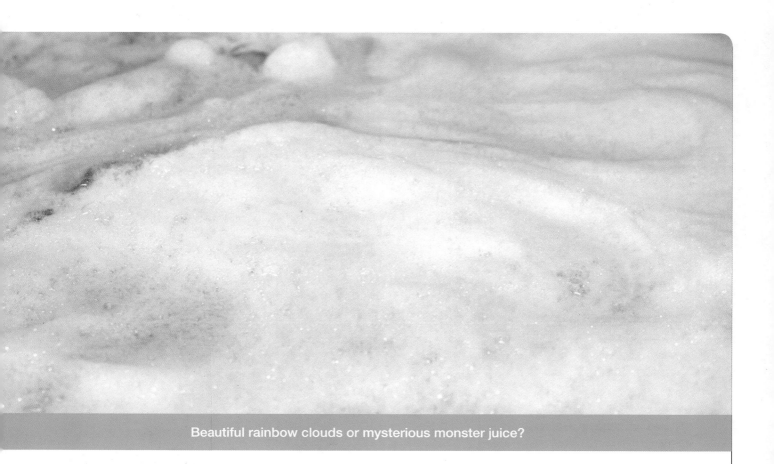

Beautiful rainbow clouds or mysterious monster juice?

Colourful foam

Targeted areas of learning:
Expressive Arts and Design
and Understanding the World

 **"It's so light. I can scoop
up lots and hold it."**

Setting up the provision

Method

Add baby bath and food colouring to a bucket with a
small amount of water in it. Mix vigorously so that you
create a foam with hardly any water left. Scoop the foam
out and place onto a builder's tray or similar. Repeat to
create different coloured foam.

Resources

- Baby bath or shampoo
- Food colouring
- Water
- Builder's tray
- Bucket
- Hand whisk or fork.

Handy hints

- If you use too much water the foam will slide around
  on the tray and quickly disappear.

- Add bowls, scoops and and ice cream tubs to create
  an ice cream factory.

Questions to help you extend the activity and to ensure challenge

Questions for you:

- Are there any stories that could link to this activity or
  could the foam inspire children to write their own stories?

- Are there opportunities for the children to top up the
  foam by creating it themselves?

How the activity can support children's development across the 7 areas of learning

Areas of Learning: Communication and Language

Children have the opportunity to:

- Describe the appearance, texture and smell of the resources.
- Make predictions.

Areas of Learning: Physical Development

Children have the opportunity to:

- Manipulate materials to achieve a planned effect.

Areas of Learning: Personal, Social and Emotional Development

Children have the opportunity to:

- Share ideas and express own opinions.
- Seek delight in new experiences.

Areas of Learning: Literacy

Children have the opportunity to:

- Mark make in the foam.
- Develop a narrative to explain where the foam has come from.

Areas of Learning: Mathematics

Children have the opportunity to:

- Use mathematical language to describe weight and size.
- Explore capacity.

Areas of Learning: Understanding the World

Children have the opportunity to:

- Comment on and describe the changes to the bubbles over time.
- Experiment with ways to create more foam.

Areas of Learning: Expressive Arts and Design

Children have the opportunity to:

- Explore and describe the texture, smell and appearance of the foam.

Look at the effects of air on the bubbles in the foam

Questions for the children:

- What does the foam remind you of?

- How do you think the foam was formed?

- What do you think will happen if we add more water to the foam?

  "The bubbles are all sparkly. You can see different rainbow colours in them."

  "I've made a marshmallow monster."

How does the activity enable children to develop and demonstrate the characteristics of effective learning?

Characteristic of effective learning	The enabling environment: Colourful foam
Playing and exploring – engagement • Finding out and exploring. • Playing with what they know. • Being willing to 'have a go'.	The activity is open-ended and multi-sensory. The appearance of the activity will draw children to try it out and 'have a go'.
Active learning – motivation • Being involved and concentrating. • Keeping trying. • Enjoying achieving what they set out to do.	Children can look closely at the detail of the bubbles. Their curiosity will open up opportunities for extended dialogue.
Creating and thinking critically – thinking • Having their own ideas. • Making links. • Choosing ways to do things.	Children can make predictions about what will happen to the bubbles over time. Children can make links with stories and develop a narrative to go alongside their exploration.

Sculpt, shape, mould. What could you create?

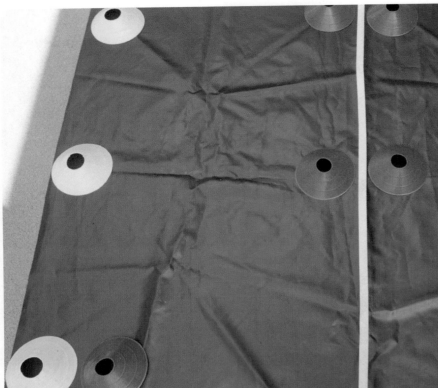
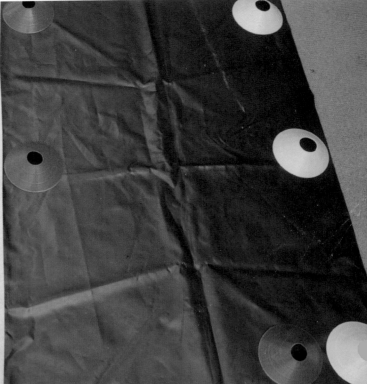

Large scale maths is often more appealing and more accessible

Symmetry

Setting up the provision

Method

Use masking tape to make a line of symmetry on the ground and set up cones either side to make a symmetrical pattern, modelling the intended outcome. Have an adult supporting children at this activity to begin with and then take time to observe how they work independently and with their peers.

Resources

- Large coloured cones or discs
- Masking tape
- A plain surface.

Handy hints

- Limit the number and colour of cones available to begin with so that the task is manageable.

- Introduce more than one colour cone as children become more confident.

Questions to help you extend the activity and to ensure challenge

Questions for you:

- Are there large 2D shapes available that you could exchange for the cones?

- Are there opportunities for children to record their patterns?

Questions for the children:

- Can you explain your pattern? Can you talk about the colours and shapes you have used?

"This one needs to be close to the line."

How does the activity enable children to develop and demonstrate the characteristics of effective learning?

Characteristic of effective learning	The enabling environment: Symmetry
Playing and exploring – engagement ● Finding out and exploring. ● Playing with what they know. ● Being willing to 'have a go'.	The activity is on a large scale, providing greater opportunity for working collaboratively with others.
Active learning – motivation ● Being involved and concentrating. ● Keeping trying. ● Enjoying achieving what they set out to do.	Children can enjoy pride and success as they achieve the end goal. Children have the opportunity to demonstrate high levels of concentration.
Creating and thinking critically – thinking ● Having their own ideas. ● Making links. ● Choosing ways to do things.	Children will need to work strategically and develop problem solving skills. Children will need to listen and respond to the ideas of others.

The PE cones could also be used as 'sound buzzers' for phonics activities

How the activity can support children's development across the 7 areas of learning

Areas of Learning: Communication and Language
Children have the opportunity to:
- Widen their vocabulary.
- Describe new concepts.

Areas of Learning: Physical Development
Children have the opportunity to:
- Develop spatial awareness.
- Work on a larger scale.

Areas of Learning: Personal, Social and Emotional Development
Children have the opportunity to:
- Work cooperatively to solve a problem.

Areas of Learning: Literacy
Children have the opportunity to:
- Record their patterns.

Areas of Learning: Mathematics
Children have the opportunity to:
- Make a symmetrical pattern.
- Make a repeating pattern.
- Copy a pattern.
- Use positional language.

Areas of Learning: Understanding the World
Children have the opportunity to:
- Comment on features of their immediate environment.

Areas of Learning: Expressive Arts and Design
Children have the opportunity to:
- Make patterns.

- What does symmetrical mean?

- Can you find any symmetrical patterns in the environment around us?

  "Let's make it harder with more cones."

 "Put the green one next to the red one."

Working methodically to create a symmetrical pattern

Provision inspiration

Setting up an outstanding learning environment is a creative process. Inspiration for this environment should be drawn from many different sources.

Build up a bank of essentials

Building up a bank of staple resources will make adapting activities even easier. Suggested staple resources:

- Coloured sand
- Collection of rocks and stones
- Shells
- Plants
- Assorted sized containers
- Paint
- Glitter
- Clipboards
- Writing tools
- Old cuts of different coloured fabric.

Many of these can be sourced at low cost or for free!

Adapt what has worked well in the past

If an activity has proved popular with children in the past then use this as the basis for a new activity. Often by just changing one element of the provision you can achieve a completely new scene. For example, Desert life (page 52) could easily be transformed into an English garden simply by changing the colour of the sand.

Original provision	Adapted provision
Desert life	Swap the orange sand for green sand, add some fresh leaves and you are in an English garden.
Potions lab	Add some washing up liquid and bottles to create a fizzy drinks factory.
Arctic freeze	Remove the animals, add some silver foil and rocks and you are on the moon.

Conclusion

You can also...

Visit other settings

Sharing good practice is an excellent way of generating new ideas. When you visit other settings, always ask if you can take photos. You can then recreate and personalise these activities for your own classroom over time.

Observe children's interests

Observing children's interests closely will enable you to plan meaningful and engaging activities. For example, observing monster role play calls for slime, caves and hazard tape. Excitement about Christmas calls for arctic scenes and map making for Santa's important deliveries.

Use a story book

Use a popular book to tie your activities together. Create small world scenes based on the setting and set up art activities to create story props.

Ask the children!

The best source of ideas will always come from the children themselves; after all they are at the heart of the environment. Always ask them what they would like to have in each area of the classroom and allow them to help set up the activities where possible.

Acknowledgements

Acknowledgement goes to the staff at Cathedral Primary School. A dedicated team who do all that they can to ensure children thrive in an exciting and inspiring environment.

An enormous 'thank you' goes to the children at Cathedral School who teach the adults new things every day!

Thanks also to the setting, team and parents for permission to use these photos. Thank you to the children for their quotes used in the book.

How does the activity enable children to develop and demonstrate the characteristics of effective learning? (Fill in below)

Characteristic of effective learning	The enabling environment: _____
Playing and exploring – engagement ● Finding out and exploring. ● Playing with what they know. ● Being willing to 'have a go'.	
Active learning – motivation ● Being involved and concentrating. ● Keeping trying. ● Enjoying achieving what they set out to do.	
Creating and thinking critically – thinking ● Having their own ideas. ● Making links. ● Choosing ways to do things.	

7 areas of learning table

How the activity can support children's development across the 7 areas of learning

Areas of Learning: Communication and Language

Children have the opportunity to:

-
-
-

Areas of Learning: Physical Development

Children have the opportunity to:

-
-
-

Areas of Learning: Personal, Social and Emotional Development

Children have the opportunity to:

-
-
-

Areas of Learning: Literacy

Children have the opportunity to:

-
-
-

Areas of Learning: Mathematics

Children have the opportunity to:

-
-
-

Areas of Learning: Understanding the World

Children have the opportunity to:

-
-
-

Areas of Learning: Expressive Arts and Design

Children have the opportunity to:

-
-
-